THE TOXICITY OF ME
LORD, DON'T LET ME BE TOXIC

PASTOR BRIDGETTE HILL

WATCH THOSE WHO HAVE TO MAKE YOU
LOOK LITTLE TO MAKE THEMSELVES LOOK BIG!

WESTBOW
PRESS®
A DIVISION OF THOMAS NELSON
& ZONDERVAN

WestBow Press books may be ordered through booksellers or by contacting:

WestBow Press
A Division of Thomas Nelson & Zondervan
1663 Liberty Drive
Bloomington, IN 47403
www.westbowpress.com
844-714-3454

ISBN: 978-1-6642-5544-9 (sc)
ISBN: 978-1-6642-5545-6 (hc)
ISBN: 978-1-6642-5543-2 (e)

Library of Congress Control Number: 2022901003

Print information available on the last page.

WestBow Press rev. date: 04/06/2022

DEDICATION

This book is dedicated to my family and friends, who were never too tired or occupied to listen. You allowed me to vent, cry, and express myself without judgment. Because there are so many people who do not have the outlets I was blessed to have, I am writing this book for them. I want them to know that deliverance from self is indeed possible no matter how the toxicity entered their lives.

Ms. Hill is intentional!

I purposely wrote this book with extra spaces between each line so you can add notes. Please get a red pen (ballpoint only) and add what the Lord gives you. If you see there are things that need to be changed and/or addressed in your life, highlight the issue with your pen as you read and assess your actions.

The goal is to make you take a closer look at your actions as well as those you interact with to become a better you.

I AM TOXIC.

AM I TOXIC?

THEY ARE TOXIC, NOT ME.

I AM TOXIC, NOT THEM.

HE DID IT

THEY DID IT

Lord, please don't let me be toxic but a blessing.

CONTENTS

INTRODUCTION

Let all bitterness and wrath and anger and clamor and
slander be put away from you, along with all malice.
Be kind to one another, tenderhearted, forgiving
one another, as God in Christ forgave you.

—Ephesians 4:31–32

Have you ever been around people who made you sick? You talk
to them and walk away feeling as if they have opened a trash
bag filled with stinky, smelly, rotten trash and poured it on you.
I have been around people so negative I feel like I need to take a
bath because they are so heavy. These people are toxic!

Everything they say is negative. They find ways to attack you
every chance they get. They say ugly things to get a laugh at
your expense. Toxic! You are the butt of every joke. There are
people who will embarrass you publicly. These people will dog

you out in public to make themselves look grand, which means important, wonderful, and fascinating. Toxic!

Life Nugget

If people have to make you look little
to make themselves look big or better,
they are dealing with insecurities of
their own. Let me say this to you,
"Run! They are not your friends."

These people hate or can't stand anyone else. They have an opinion on everything, and the majority of their opinions and comments are negative.

Can You Say "Toxic"?

It is my prayer that we take a good look at ourselves to see if we have toxic tendencies. Ask yourself these questions:

1. When I speak, do I *say negative things* most of the time?
2. When I think, do I *think negative thoughts* most of the time?
3. When I am at work, do my coworkers *come to me or run from me?*

4. When I am at work, am I looked at as someone with a *bad attitude or someone who is pleasant to be around?*

5. When I am with my family, I am viewed *as someone my family wants to see come home,* or am I viewed as someone *they hate to see come home?*

6. When you meet with your friends, are you discussing *negative things most of the time?*

7. How do you feel *after leaving those conversations?*

8. Do you feel drained when negative people leave you?

It's always something … blah, blah, blah.

Toxic people are defined as anyone who is abusive, unsupportive, or emotionally unhealthy. They bring you down more than up. If you are not careful, you may begin to doubt your own opinions because theirs tend to override yours. They want you to think like them.

POINT 1

Toxic People Are Manipulative

Make no friendship with a man given to anger,
nor go with a wrathful man, lest you learn his
ways and entangle yourself in a snare.

—Proverbs 22:24–25

Toxic people work to change your way of thinking. They want to persuade you to do things their way. They will even trick you into doing the things they want to see done. Beware: If you're not careful, you will find yourself moving more their way than yours.

> But understand this, that in the last days there will come times of difficulty. For people will be lovers of self, lovers of money, proud, arrogant, abusive, disobedient to their parents, ungrateful, unholy, heartless, unappeasable, slanderous, without self-control, brutal, not loving good, treacherous, reckless, swollen with conceit, lovers of pleasure rather than lovers of God, having the appearance of godliness, but denying its power. Avoid such people. (2 Timothy 3:1–5)

> And Jesus answered them, "See that no one leads you astray." (Matthew 24:4)

You should watch the company you keep. I suggest you refresh your contact list annually. The same people should not be in your address book from five years ago. Some people will be but not all because we grow differently. You should not be on the same level spiritually as you were five years ago.

Manipulator Defined

A manipulator is a person who seeks to create an imbalance of power and take advantage of someone to gain power, control, benefits, and/or privileges at the expense of the victim. Manipulation is defined as any attempt to sway someone's emotions to get them to act or feel a certain way.

Manipulators use the needs of others as leverage for one's agenda. They may even pretend to be kind and good, helpful and trustworthy while gaining the upper hand for ulterior motives.

Delilah was the queen of manipulation. She worked with spies to discover the secret of Samson's strength, which was his hair. Because this manipulator was relentless, she got what she wanted. Please note that although Samson fell by being in the hands of the manipulator, God prevailed. Let us look at the Word of God:

> After this he loved a woman in the Valley of Sorek, whose name was Delilah. And the lords of the Philistines came up to her and said to her, "Seduce him, and see where his great strength lies, and by what means we may overpower him, that we may bind him to humble him. And we will each give you 1,100 pieces of silver." So Delilah said to Samson, "Please tell me where your great strength lies, and how you might be bound, that one could subdue you."

Samson said to her, "If they bind me with seven fresh bowstrings that have not been dried, then I shall become weak and be like any other man." Then the lords of the Philistines brought up to her seven fresh bowstrings that had not been dried, and she bound him with them. Now she had men lying in ambush in an inner chamber. And she said to him, "The Philistines are upon you, Samson!" But he snapped the bowstrings, as a thread of flax snaps when it touches the fire. So the secret of his strength was not known.

Then Delilah said to Samson, "Behold, you have mocked me and told me lies. Please tell me how you might be bound." And he said to her, "If they bind me with new ropes that have not been used, then I shall become weak and be like any other man." So Delilah took new ropes and bound him with them and said to him, "The Philistines are upon you, Samson!" And the men lying in ambush were in an inner chamber. But he snapped the ropes off his arms like a thread.

Then Delilah said to Samson, "Until now you have mocked me and told me lies. Tell me how you might be bound." And he said to her, "If you weave the seven locks of my head with the web and fasten it tight with the pin, then I shall become weak and be like any other man." So while he slept, Delilah took the seven locks of his head and wove them into the web.[a] And she made them tight with the pin and said to him, "The Philistines are upon you, Samson!" But he awoke from his sleep and pulled away the pin, the loom, and the web.

And she said to him, "How can you say, 'I love you,' when your heart is not with me? You have mocked me these three times, and you have not told me where your great strength lies." And when she pressed him hard with her words day after day, and urged him, his soul was vexed to death. And he told her all his heart, and said to her, "A razor has never come upon my head, for I have been a Nazirite to God from my mother's womb. If my head is shaved, then my strength will leave me, and I shall become weak and be like any other man."

When Delilah saw that he had told her all his heart, she sent and called the lords of the Philistines, saying, "Come up again, for he has told me all his heart." Then the lords of the Philistines came up to her and brought the money in their hands.

She made him sleep on her knees. And she called a man and had him shave off the seven locks of his head. Then she began to torment him, and his strength left him. And she said, "The Philistines are upon you, Samson!" And he awoke from his sleep and said, "I will go out as at other times and shake myself free." But he did not know that the Lord had left him. (Judges 16:4–20)

Samson knew he was dealing with a manipulator. So why he would toy with Delilah is beyond me. Ask God to identify the manipulators in your life. Then ask God to remove them or give you the strength to walk away.

Father, I confess ...

_____

_____

_____

_____

_____

_____

_____

_____

_____

_____

_____

_____

_____

_____

_____

_____

_____

_____

_____

_____

_____

_____

Dear Heavenly Father,

Thank you for helping me to see that I have been toxic in the area of manipulation. I renounce everything I set in motion that is not of you. Forgive me for not putting you first. Forgive me for being manipulative, domineering, and intrusive. Forgive me for being upset with others for not doing things the way I thought they should have been done. Please remove the spirit of manipulation from me. Remove toxic, hurtful words from my mouth. Restore me as only you can. In Jesus' name, Amen.

POINT 2

Toxic People Are Judgmental

A fool takes no pleasure in understanding,
but only in expressing his opinion.

—Proverbs 18:2

Judge not, that you be not judged. For with the
judgment, you pronounce you will be judged, and with
the measure you use it will be measured to you.

—Matthew 7:1–5

Toxic people love to judge people. They are very opinionated. It is their way or no way at all! There is no compromise, no middle ground. They can be quick to speak judgment over others. They believe in doom and gloom. They are the judge and jury.

> Do not be deceived: God is not mocked, for whatever
> one sows, that will he also reap. (Galatians 6:7)

Galatians 6:7 simply means if you sow negativity, you will reap negativity. If you sow kindness, you will reap kindness. Yes, you will reap what you sow. Remember, what goes around comes around. Are you getting the point? I have heard people make statements such as, "Her daughter is so fast, she's gonna have a bunch of babies," or, "Their son ain't nothing but a loser." In both instances, those comments came back to bite them in the butt. Everything that was said about other people came back on them. Yes, it happened to them! Another saying I grew up hearing was, "Don't throw stones if you live in a glass house." This saying is a quote from Benjamin Franklin which dates back to the early 1700's. It means that one who is vulnerable to criticism regarding a certain issue should not criticize others about the same issue. There is only one true judge, and that is God. The same God who was good enough for Mama and Grandma is good today and is still keeping us. When I get through handling my own business, I do not have the time to mind someone else's. Simply put, mind your business and leave others alone.

I think everyone should think about what I am saying. I can attest to the fact that the energy given to the business of others can be used to start a business, generate wealth, or even write a book. When you are talking about others, sharing their details and sizing them up, you are sitting in a seat you are not qualified to sit in. It's called the judgment seat.

> Judge not, that you be not judged. For with the judgment you pronounce you will be judged, and with the measure you use it will be measured to you. Why do you see the speck that is in your brother's eye, but do not notice the log that is in your own eye? Or how can you say to your brother, "Let me take the speck out of your eye," when there is the log in your own eye? You hypocrite, first take the log out of your own eye, and then you will see clearly to take the speck out of your brother's eye. (Matthew 7:1–5)

Jesus asks, "Why do you see the speck that is in your brother's eye," but do not see the log in yours? (Matthew 7:3) It's easy to point out the flaws and issues of others. You see what they are not doing. We accuse others of misconduct. And when we judge, we do not realize that we are losing points with God too. So instead, ask God to reveal and heal the flaws in you.

Father, I confess ...

_____

_____

_____

_____

_____

_____

_____

_____

_____

_____

_____

_____

_____

_____

_____

_____

_____

_____

_____

Dear Heavenly Father,

Please forgive me as I am guilty of being judgmental. Forgive me for putting my mouth on others. I renounce everything I said about them. Forgive me for calling out others and spreading gossip about them. Forgive me for pushing my negative opinions. Please remove the spirit of judgment from me. According to your Word, you are the *only* righteous judge. You love justice, and the upright will see your face. So I do not have the right to sit in the seat that belongs to you. Please remove this toxic behavior from me. Restore me as only you can. In Jesus' name, Amen.

POINT 3

Toxic People Shift Blame

Toxic people love to play the blame game. They take no responsibility for their actions. You can ask why something was not done, and instead of receiving a clear answer, you get a list of excuses as to why it did not occur. All they really have to say is, "I am sorry that I failed to get it done. However, I can hop on it now." Just admit that it was not done. This is a pet peeve of mine. I have no respect for those who can never give a solid answer instead of a tub of unwelcomed, unsolicited excuses for incomplete tasks. In the time it took for them to conjure up lies or lists their excuses, they could have completed the task. These toxic people love to shift blame.

And it's nothing new. In Genesis 3, we find that the blame game is played. Adam blamed Eve, and Eve blamed the snake (serpent). Ultimately, everyone was punished. One might wonder what would have happened had they not shifted the blame but instead came clean and apologized for their disobedience. Adam was given a task to watch and tend the garden.

> The Lord God took the man and put him in the Garden of Eden to work it and take care of it. And the Lord God commanded the man, "You are free to eat from any tree in the garden; but you must not eat from the tree of the knowledge of good and evil, for when you eat from it you will certainly die." (Genesis 2:15–17)

After God gives Adam clear instructions regarding the tree, the creation of woman—Eve—happens. God feels that man should not be alone:

> Then the Lord God said, "It is not good that the man should be alone; I will make him a helper fit for him." Now out of the ground the Lord God had formed every beast of the field and every bird of the heavens and brought them to the man to see what he would call them. And whatever the man called every living creature, that was its name. The man gave names to all livestock and to the birds of the heavens and to every beast of the field. But for Adam there was not found a helper fit for him. So the Lord God caused a deep sleep to fall upon the man, and while he slept took one of his ribs and closed up its place with flesh. And the rib that the Lord God had taken from the man he made into a woman and brought her to the man. Then the man said,
>
> "This at last is bone of my bones and flesh of my flesh; she shall be called Woman, because she was taken out of Man." (Genesis 18–23)

Please note that she did not have a name at this point. She is referred to as woman.

> Therefore a man shall leave his father and his mother and hold fast to his wife, and they shall become one flesh. And the man and his wife were both naked and were not ashamed. (Genesis 2:18–25)

Now we move to Genesis chapter 3, which opens with how cunning the snake is. The snake has begun to converse with the woman (Eve), convincing her to go against God.

> Now the serpent was more crafty than any other beast of the field that the LORD God had made. He said to the woman, "Did God actually say, 'You shall not eat of any tree in the garden'?"(Genesis 3:3)

Now at some point there is a conversation between Adam and the woman because the serpent is aware that she knows what she can and cannot eat:

> And the woman said to the serpent, "We may eat of the fruit of the trees in the garden, but God said, 'You shall not eat of the fruit of the tree that is in the midst of the garden, neither shall you touch it, lest you die.'" But the serpent said to the woman, "You will not surely die. For God knows that when you eat of it your eyes will be

opened, and you will be like God, knowing good and evil." (Genesis 3:2–5)

Life Nugget

Watch snake talk! She should not have been talking to a snake in the first place.

Eve, what were you thinking?

So when the woman saw that the tree was good for food, and that it was a delight to the eyes, and that the tree was to be desired to make one wise, she took of its fruit and ate, and she also gave some to her husband who was with her, and he ate. (Genesis 3:6)

This part of the story has always bothered me. Adam does not question Eve once he is presented with the fruit. You do not find in scripture that Adam says, "Eve, where have you been?" There is no, "Eve, where did you get this fruit?" Instead, he sees that she has taken a bite of the fruit and feels it is okay to eat after her. Adam does not consider that the results of her actions would show up later. Why? Because he is oblivious to the fact that she obtained the fruit from the tree from which he was instructed not to eat.

Then the eyes of both were opened, and they knew that they were naked. And they sewed fig leaves together and made themselves loincloths. And they heard the sound of the Lord God walking in the garden in the cool of the day, and the man and his wife hid themselves from the presence of the Lord God among the trees of the garden. But the Lord God called to the man and said to him, "Where are you?" And he said, "I heard the sound of you in the garden, and I was afraid, because I was naked, and I hid myself." He said, "Who told you that you were naked? Have you eaten of the tree of which I commanded you not to eat?" The man said, "The woman whom you gave to be with me, she gave me fruit of the tree, and I ate." Then the Lord God said to the woman, "What is this that you have done?" The woman said, "The serpent deceived me, and I ate." The Lord God said to the serpent, "Because you have done this, cursed are you above all livestock and above all beasts of the field; on your belly you shall go, and dust you shall eat all the days of your life. I will put enmity between you and the woman, and between your offspring and her offspring; he shall bruise your head, and you shall bruise his heel."

To the woman he said,

"I will surely multiply your pain in childbearing; in pain you shall bring forth children. Your desire shall be contrary to your husband, but he shall rule over you." And to Adam he said,

"Because you have listened to the voice of your wife and have eaten of the tree of which I commanded you, 'You shall not eat of it,' cursed is the ground because of you; in pain you shall eat of it all the days of your life; thorns and thistles it shall bring forth for you; and you shall eat the plants of the field. By the sweat of your face you shall eat bread, till you return to the ground, for out of it you were taken; for you are dust, and to dust you shall return." (Genesis 7–19)

Told ya! This was not going to end well. A toxic person will always say it was someone else's fault. They will always say they didn't do this or that because of this reason and/or that reason. They make up stories to cover their butts. They give 101 reasons why something else interfered with doing the task they were chosen to do. Be careful when you are dealing with anyone who will not take responsibility for his or her own actions. I would be even willing to step out on a limb and say to *expect* a lie amid what they are telling you. The truth of the matter is that toxic people are afraid of facing the fallout for their failures to act.

> For each will have to bear his own load.
> (Galatians 6:5)

Father, I confess ...

_____

_____

_____

_____

_____

_____

_____

_____

_____

_____

_____

_____

_____

_____

_____

_____

_____

_____

_____

_____

_____

_____

_____

Dear Heavenly Father,

Forgive me for playing the blame game. I am sorry for not taking responsibility for my actions. I am sorry that I have not acted in integrity as I should. Thank you for helping me to see where I have fallen short in the toxic area of shifting blame. Please remove this toxic behavior. Forgive me for making excuses instead of completing the task. Help me to take responsibility for my actions. I realize that I am a hindrance (liability) not a help (asset) by continuing this behavior. Today I will be open and honest when an assignment is given. I will first work to see it through, but if I see that I am overwhelmed and cannot complete the task on time, I will not set false expectations. Instead, I will communicate with the person in charge. I will be upfront, open, and honest about my workload; I will be honest with myself and my capabilities, understanding that the goal is to get it done in a timely manner. In Jesus' name, Amen.

POINT 4

Toxic People Don't Apologize

For those people who feel like they do not need to apologize, I beg to differ. These toxic people who are too arrogant to apologize. They are honorary. The Bible tells us in 1 Peter 5:6 to humble ourselves under the hand of the Almighty that he may exalt you in due time. Some people cannot be exalted to the place God desires because they refuse to confess, apologize, or simply come clean. Toxic people feel entitled and believe they do not have to apologize because in their minds, they are never wrong. However, these same arrogant people will expect an apology from you. Wait, what?

Toxic individuals feel like they can live how they want to live unapologetically. These people scare me the most. They feel they can do whatever they want to do, and there will be no punishment for their actions. They also believe there is no recourse. Their heartless words and twisted, disconnected ways of handling people are law. It is the take-it-or-leave-it attitude. They can be shrewd. They do not care about the lives they destroy; they will wreck your life and expect you to deal with it. They also have a keep-it-moving attitude. They are not concerned at all about the next person. It is all about them.

Agendas on this level of toxicity are very cold and calculating. In my opinion, they can also be dangerous. How can you not feel bad about destroying others? For example, there are women who will sleep with a married man without regard for the wife and kids at home. Some people will destroy churches and not give it a second thought. The Bible says, "Woa be unto them who scatter the flock" (Jeremiah 23:1). That is not at all healthy. That is very toxic!

> If we say we have no sin, we deceive ourselves, and the truth is not in us. (1 John 1:8)

> Therefore, confess your sins to one another and pray for one another, that you may be healed. The prayer of a righteous person has great power as it is working. (James 5:16)

Father, I confess ...

_____

_____

_____

_____

_____

_____

_____

_____

_____

_____

_____

_____

_____

_____

_____

_____

_____

_____

_____

_____

_____

_____

_____

Dear Heavenly Father,

Your Word says in 1 Peter 5:6 to humble ourselves under the mighty hand of God that, in due time, you will exalt us. I am sorry for not humbling myself and for not apologizing to those I offended. I am sorry for not acting in a manner that is pleasing to you. Father, your Word also teaches us to live peaceably with others. By not apologizing, I have chosen to leave things unresolved.

Lord, create in me a clean heart, and renew in me a right spirit according to Psalm 51:10. Your Word also asks how we can love you, our heavenly Father, and hate those we see every day. I do not want to continue to leave things unresolved. Help me to realize that apologies are not a sign of weakness but a sign of strength. In Jesus' name, Amen.

POINT 5

Toxic People Are Inconsistent

I nconsistent is defined as not staying the same. Individuals who are inconsistent will say one thing and do another. There are many synonyms for the word "inconsistent," including "fickle," "shy," "insipid," "spineless," "hesitant," "dillydallying," "uncertain," "infirm," "changeable," "unresolved," "watery," "shifty," "irresponsible," "undecided," "erratic," "half hearted," "unwilling," "unsure," "impulsive," "tentative," "indecisive," "fly-by-night," "undependable," and "volatile."

This type of person cannot be relied on. You cannot trust them to come through for you. They are not dependable. You just cannot trust them! When you have someone who is operating inconsistently, it is very frustrating. This toxic person lives like a yo-yo, or better yet, a roller coaster because he or she is all over the place. This type of toxic connection is very much against the biblical grain that God set for us. The Bible tells us that double-minded individuals are unstable in their ways (James 1:8). They cannot be relied on to make engagements. And forget about them being on time. They cannot be trusted to make it to the parking lot let alone to the event.

I have set up job interviews as well as performance opportunities for people, and while I wait on them to show up, they text me to say they are not coming. It was very embarrassing to say the least. My word is bond. People know that I will deliver. However, if I can't make it, I will send an alternate.

Father, I confess …

_____

_____

_____

_____

_____

_____

_____

_____

_____

_____

_____

_____

_____

_____

_____

_____

_____

_____

_____

_____

Dear Heavenly Father,

You are not the author of confusion. Forgive me for not being consistent. Forgive me for not keeping my word and for breaking promises. This toxic behavior is not of you. Your Son, Jesus, was the perfect example of how to be consistent. He did what he said he would do. Jesus came through every time. He could have aborted his mission to the cross, but he did not. He was hung up for my hang-ups, and I am truly grateful. Help me to stay focused on the tasks at hand. Help me to remember to write down my assignments. Organize me, God. When my mind begins to wander, please bring my thoughts back to submission. In Jesus' name, Amen.

POINT 6

Toxic People Are Selfish

W hat does it mean to be selfish?

It means to be concerned excessively or exclusively with oneself; seeking or concentrating on one's own advantage, pleasure, or well-being without regard for others. Someone who is selfish is unsupportive, uncaring, and not interested in what's important to you.

> Let each of you look not only to his own interests,
> but also to the interests of others. (Philippians 2:4)

If you know someone who fits this description, *run!*

But if this is you, repent. Ask God to change your way of walking, talking, thinking, and so on. Stop this insensitive behavior!

You may support someone who is selfish, but the person will never support you. The selfish person will know you are sick but not even bother to check on or cook for you. Someone who is selfish will only call if he or she needs something. Remember that the selfish person genuinely does not care about you. He or she is self-absorbed and does not care about your well-being as long as you can run and do for them. But as soon as you cannot be used by the individual, he or she will selfishly move on to the next victim. What others are going through means nothing to them.

The Bible tells us to be sober and vigilant because these toxic people truly mean us no good. Their only motives are to get what they can out of others. Just because they say they love and care for you does not make it so. It is a sad and harsh reality, but it is true and very hurtful. The selfish person will look you in the eye and tell you a lie. Why? Because this person must come up with a justification for why you have not heard from him or her.

When toxic people need or want something from others, they become the people you cannot get rid of. But as soon as you give them what they want, things go back to the way things were. You will not hear from them until they have another issue. Detox yourselves from these people. Just do not answer the phone or emails. They want to entangle you in their webs of drama. I say this again: "Run!"

Father, I confess ...

_____

_____

_____

_____

_____

_____

_____

_____

_____

_____

_____

_____

_____

_____

_____

_____

_____

_____

_____

_____

_____

_____

Dear Heavenly Father,

Please forgive me for being selfish. I am sorry for not considering the feelings of others. I am sorry for taking advantage of genuinely kindhearted people to advance myself and push my agendas. Forgive my deceptive ways. I confess that I have lied to get my way. I also confess that I made excuses to cover the fact that I neglected to act selflessly toward others.

Forgive me for not supporting others as they have supported me. Help me to demonstrate the love of your Son, Jesus, who gave his life for me. Give me a heart to love and serve your people just as Jesus did time after time. Change my way of thinking! Restore me like no one else can. In Jesus' name, Amen.

POINT 7

Toxic People Are Abusive

Y ou must be mindful of a toxic relationship, especially in this day and time. I am referring to domestic violence. I have another set of points to share with you.

Let's Define Our Terms

Physical abuse is any intentional act causing injury or trauma to another person through bodily contact.

Verbal abuse occurs when someone repeatedly uses words to demean, frighten, or control someone.

Emotional abuse can involve any of the following:

➤ Verbal abuse: yelling at you, insulting you, or swearing at you.

➤ Rejection: constantly rejecting your thoughts, ideas, and opinions.

➤ Gaslighting: Making you doubt your own feelings and thoughts, and even your sanity by manipulating the truth.

An assailant is someone who physically attacks another.

Physical abuse does not start immediately. It is a hidden evil that emerges after some time. When a person has no self-control and anger management problems, what started as verbal abuse escalates to physical abuse. These toxic people will apologize and try to justify why it occurred. Then comes the shifting of blame: "If you hadn't provoked me, I would not have done this. Baby, don't provoke me next time." These comments are made all while the victim is trying to figure out what, why, and how the assault occurred. Now the victim says, "He told me that he loved me. He said that he would let nothing happen to me. He said all of that, and now the person who is supposed to love, care, and protect me is assaulting me." If that victim does not walk away immediately after the first time, the abuse will more than likely happen again and again.

Most people feel that only men assault women. But there are many cases where women have assaulted men.

There are signs of abuse we must pay close attention to.

Sign 1: Be Mindful of Those Who Want to Pull You Away from Family and Friends

This toxic person has an agenda. Many times it is a self-serving and manipulative agenda. If he or she can isolate you, the toxic person feels able to do whatever he or she wants to do, and no one can stop it. Why? Because you belong to that person.

I thank God for my father being the strong man that he was. By the grace of God, he protected us. He provided for us. He went to work and came home faithfully. His red truck was parked in front of our yard, and people knew he was there. His presence was strong. I bless God that we did not have to wonder if he was coming home or not. My mom's saying was that Daddy, Fulton Jackson was the king, she, Arnest Jackson was the queen, my younger sister, Lisa and I were the princesses. One of the best gifts my classmate, Anthony (AD) Davis could have given me was when he said that my dad would gather the young men at lunchtime and tell them how to take care of home. I just cried because my dad did that. At our house, we ate at the same time. Daddy paid attention to us. He validated and complimented us. He gave us life lessons. Again, his presence was strong. This is a message that I preach today to the men. See, you shout and proclaim you are the king of the castle. However, how can you rule and never be there? How can you say that you are the head of the family, and the rest is left to fend for themselves? How can you protect the home when you are in someone else's bed? I'm confused. Men, please get it together! Take your rightful place and be present. Ladies, stop saying you do not need men in your lives. I'll probably say this again, but it is because of my dad's presence, things that could have occurred did not. I am truly grateful to God for his love and concern. Celebrate the men in your lives. Bottom line, we need each other.

Sign 2: Be Mindful of Those Who Are Quick Tempered

When he or she is angry, the quick-tempered person often throws things. The person likes to break things such as dishes and windows. Quick-tempered individuals are quick to call you names and say unchristian things to you. They will curse at you. They will belittle you. If they cannot have their ways, they instantly go elsewhere.

Let's see what the Bible says about these actions.

> Before man of quick temper acts foolishly, and a man of evil devices is hated. (Proverbs 14:17)

> A soft answer turns away wrath, but a harsh word stirs up anger. (Proverbs 15:1)

> For the anger of man does not produce the righteousness of God. (James 1:20)

> A fool gives full vent to his spirit, but a wise man quietly holds it back. (Proverbs 29:11)

> Whoever is slow to anger has great understanding, but he who has a hasty temper exalts folly. (Proverbs 14:29)

Abusive relations are not only toxic but potentially dangerous. The reason a toxic person wants to move you away from your family and friends is to better enable changing your thinking, surroundings, and ultimately, to change you. Why? Because the toxic person does not want the task of having to combat your family and friends who will try to rationalize with you or speak up for you. Some toxic people want you away from everybody so he or she can get away with abusing you. I will tell anyone who will listen that there is value to having brothers, a father, and other male figures in your life. Sometimes we want to keep our families and friends out of our business because they can be meddlesome. I believe in boundaries, but please keep in mind the topic under discussion here. If you are the family member and see things that are not right, now is not the time to walk away. This is the time perhaps to make more wellness checks.

Here are some examples: You could reach out to say hello every morning. You are simply creating a habit to ensure they are okay. If you are working from home, have your assistant or coworker call you at the same time daily to ensure you are good. We are talking about things to ensure you are safe and secure when you are dealing with toxic people.

When you meet someone new, introduce the person to your family and friends. Someone I dated years ago thought they were going to handle me in an inappropriate manner, but the strong presence of my father halted such actions. Oh yeah, did I tell you I have four godfathers, three who are hunters? I introduced them to my dates growing up.

When there is a male presence around, a toxic male will most often think twice before putting his hands on a woman. They do not want to, "Catch them hands," as the young people say. I am not trying to sound gangster; that's not my nature at all. But what I am saying is that it is a blessing to have people around you. If you find yourself on the island by yourself, and all friends and family members you have always communicated with are not communicating with you any longer, you must ask why. Could it be because of the toxic person you are connected to? Please find a way to put your friends and family back in your life. Someone needs to hear from and check on you. Within that network, create a safe house or secure location in case you must move immediately.

And another thing, when you are going out, always let someone know where you are. Send the location from your phone. If I have a meeting or am going out to dinner, I always let two or three people know. These are basic safety dating and early-relationship suggestions.

Toxic behavior alert! Women can be abusive too. Why does she not want your mother, sisters, and cousins around? Truth be told, some women in our families can be nosey and messy. I get it, but for the sake of this toxicity book, ask the questions. Why is she isolating you? You must be careful as well! No one should be isolated from family and friends in the normal scheme of things.

When I worked at a banking call center, I received a call from a young lady claiming to be the fiancée of one of our clients. Come to find out, she was very toxic. He had not put her on his bank account at that time, and she was calling to get his banking information. She claimed that "their" cards were stolen, and new cards needed to be sent out. I immediately smelled a rat. I called him, but he was at work and could not get away. I left a detailed voicemail with my direct phone number to call me back.

Shortly, after I received a call from this young man's mother who said, "I'm calling because my son is at work and cannot talk at this time. He asked me to call for him." She went on to say that the young lady (his fiancée) who called earlier stole his bank card and was trying to get banking information. After that call, I received a call from the young man himself. He called and verified the story. He said, "I apologize. I asked my mother to call you because I was at work and could not get away." He confirmed that his fiancée had stolen his bank card. It was his mother who caught her. They were waiting to see what she would do with the card. Of course, I was dying to see how this would play out. He was upset; he didn't want to believe the woman he loved would try to commit bank fraud or theft. He said, "Because my fiancée has done this, there will be no wedding." He had me block his bank card, which his fiancée still had in her possession, and reissue another card to be overnighted to his mother's house. He told me he was going to give his fiancé total access to his bank accounts. But because she jumped the gun and did not trust him to put her on his accounts, the relationship was over. He said, "I will not marry anyone I can't trust."

Well, a few minutes later Yep, you guessed it! The fiancée called, fussing and cussing! She said it was his evil mother who caused this mess. She genuinely believed that she would have gotten away with it had the messy mother stayed out of his life. Truth be told, his mother saved his money and her son from a toxic relationship.

Again, let me be clear. I do not think that family members should interfere in the marriages of others. Do I think that families in the general scheme of things should stay connected? Yes! You never know who you might need. I thank God that my mother set this family rule for us. It does not matter who you are married to, where you live, or what you do in life. When a member of your immediate family calls, we answer. Saying, "She's busy or too sick to talk," is a no-no in my family. That's the family rule! Mom does not believe in meddling in our lives, but she is going to check on us if it's to hear our voices for thirty seconds or thirty minutes. We communicate. We all check on each other.

Sign 3: They Want to Keep You Financially Dependent on Them

Keep your finances straight. An abuser wants to keep you incapacitated by keeping you broke. I worked with a woman many years ago who told me that her husband was a very mean man with a drinking problem. Her marriage was very toxic to say the least. Let us just say that makeup cannot cover everything. Every paycheck she would go to the bank and get twenty to forty dollars in quarters. She put them in a shoebox in her closet. Whenever she needed money for food, gas, or a hotel room to get away, she would grab her quarters, throw the amount she needed in the bag, and go. She had done this for many years, and he never found out about her safety money. For my male readers, this can work for you too.

Father, I confess …

_____

_____

_____

_____

_____

_____

_____

_____

_____

_____

_____

_____

_____

_____

_____

_____

_____

_____

_____

_____

Dear Heavenly Father,

Please forgive me for having an abusive nature. I confess to having anger issues, not being able to control my emotions. Whether my issue is generational or started with me, this day I repent and decree and declare in the name of Jesus it all stops here. Forgive me for putting my hands on someone, cursing, fighting, demeaning the person or people in my life, past and present. Please, Father, I admit that I have a problem only you can solve. I surrender my will and way to you.

I need to be healed in the area of perception. I perceive people in ways that make me superior or dominant, which is not of you. You are my God, Creator, and Ruler of my life. You are my Savior and my strength. I submit to you. I do not have the right to make anyone fear me. I do not have the right to make anyone want to hide from me because he or she is afraid of my reactions. I am truly sorry for my ways. I ask that you reconcile me and whomever I have hurt physically, emotionally, or verbally through the blood of Jesus according to the Word of God (Colossians 1:20).

Open my heart to receive or pursue the help I need to deal with the real issues inside me. Open my heart to accept the changes, so my life and the lives of others can be changed. Restore me like no one else can. In Jesus' name, Amen.

POINT 8

Toxic People Are Controlling

Controlling people make you feel like you have no opinions. They want to change you into what they think you should be. These toxic people try to snuff out your dreams and plans, and they love to create drama, criticize you, and treat you like a child. They desire to take your power—the power you have to make decisions on your own and the power to think freely.

When someone tries to take your voice from you, this is not good at all. When someone wants to control your thoughts and dominate you, please know that is not of God. God gave us free will.

So why would it be okay for someone to force himself or herself on you and God when our Creator has not? Think about that for a minute. Does the person you are talking to make you feel extremely heavy? Do you feel like your thoughts are bound or handcuffed?

If so, this is not of God!

I met a nice man around my fiftieth birthday. The initial conversations were wonderful. He had potential, so I thought. There was a shift in his demeanor by our third conversation. He became very negative, aggressive, and dark. He had issues with everything and everyone. I began to have headaches and started feeling sick at just the thought of him. My heart would race, but not in the way it does when love grows. I knew that he had to go.

There were no ifs or buts about it. This guy wanted to change my thinking. Correction: He wanted to *dominate* my thinking. If I said something, he would stop me and correct the way I said it. If I made a blanket statement, it was scrutinized and dissected. By then I was thinking, *I am educated. I have a bachelor's degree. I am a retired banker. I had clients in and out of the country. I dealt with millionaires daily. I am very astute. I am established. Through the grace of God, I am living very comfortably. I am financially sound and I am putting up with this. Why?* I realized that the Holy Spirit was letting me know that he was not the one for me, and he had to go immediately. Do not ignore the signs. The headaches and the immediate sickness that occurred at the thought of him were huge signs that he had something bad going on within. I asked him about church. He would decline. He was in sales, and if there was an opportunity to make money at church, he would go. Otherwise, he was busy. I want the man in my life to love God more than he loves me, so he will know how to treat me.

Life Nugget

If your significant other is too busy
for God, they are too busy for you.

Husbands, love your wives, as Christ loved the church and gave himself up for her. (Ephesians 5:25)

Life Nugget

When you meet someone, do not be
quick to invite him or her to your home.
Give it time to see who you are dealing
with. Seek the Holy Spirit for guidance.

When you are dealing with that toxic personality, is the spirit of God telling you that he or she is not the person for you? Are you or have you been ignoring the signs?

Ask yourself if this person is treating you like the king or queen you are.

Let me be clear ...

I am not a male basher; there are women who will fight men. There are women who will embarrass or belittle a man anywhere. Just as a man will stalk a woman, so will a woman stalk a man. This is not one-sided. I do not believe in breaking up marriages. I did not allow anyone to break up mine. However, I advise you to leave a situation that could potentially kill you.

Father, I confess …

_____

_____

_____

_____

_____

_____

_____

_____

_____

_____

_____

_____

_____

_____

_____

_____

_____

_____

_____

Dear Heavenly Father,

Please forgive me for being controlling. I am sorry for imposing my thoughts on others. Forgive me for disregarding the feelings and opinions of others. Help me to realize that things will not always go my way. Help me to realize that I should not criticize the choices of others. Help me also to realize that I am not the only one with dreams and goals. Teach me to help others along the way. Prick my heart when I get upset with others for having opinions that do not match mine. Help me to realize that just as you gave me free will, you gave it to others as well. Restore me as only you can. In Jesus' name, Amen.

POINT 9

Toxic People Go from Relationship to Relationship

THE TOXICITY OF ME

o not set yourself up. Watch who you vent to. Because you vented and complained about the old toxic guy to the new toxic guy, the new guy will gather information and study and plan how to enter your life subtly. Sometimes he will just enter your life abruptly and overwhelm you with kind words and flattery. He or she announces, "I am the person to solve all your problems. I am the one you've been looking for," not giving you a chance to think about whether you really want to be with him or her. You call your friends to tell them that the new person in your life understands you, really understands you. You tell your friends how wonderful and amazing the person is. Remember, it was the snake in Genesis that got Adam and Eve put out of The Garden. The enemy's game is to overtake you, and before you know it, the enemy is in your home and in your life. The toxic person is now a problem you must deal with. Your abilities to breathe, think, and process have been compromised.

Some toxic people are negative because of past hurts. Someone set them off in a past relationship, and now you have to pay the price because that woman or man cheated. Now you are their punching bag. You walk into a relationship with a cow load of stipulations all because of what someone else did. Instead of getting healed or seeking spiritual or medical counsel, the person moves on quickly to another relationship. Watch the individual because he or she comes with lots of unwanted, unsolicited, and smelly baggage. He or she wants to dump it on your front lawn and say, "Here I am!" You must go through all their crazy tendencies and -isms because the person was not healed first. Now the toxic person has chosen to connect to you. They have chosen to pull and drain you. You are now responsible for making them happy when that should never be your assignment in the first place. If we would only seek God first and not move on emotions, God would tell us if others needed to be healed or not.

If this is going to be a big job for you, God will show you what you need to know—but only if you seek God first. But we often hook up first and ask God later. This is not the order of God. The Bible says, "But seek ye first the kingdom of God, and his righteousness; and all these things shall be added unto you (Matthew 6:33). Here is a simple formula: Seek God first, live right, and all shall be added.

If there are abandonment issues, they need to be addressed. If there are abuse issues, whether this person is the abuser or the person being abused, there should be some type of help. Seek professional counseling, be it from your pastor, a psychiatrist, or a psychologist. Please know that it is okay to seek help. Lying on someone's couch is not embarrassing. It is not a bad thing; it is healthy.

If you are not careful, you will sell yourself short, thinking that you are ready for something that you are honestly not ready for at all. All you are doing is trying to fill a void because you do not want to be lonely. The truth is that you are honestly invading someone else's space and peace. The person trying to help you will find himself or herself in an exhausting situation; that person thought he or she could take on the highs and lows of you. Soon the person will realize he or she is not qualified to deal with your level of toxicity, complexities, depression, vulnerabilities, and your-isms.

Father, I confess …

_____

_____

_____

_____

_____

_____

_____

_____

_____

_____

_____

_____

_____

_____

_____

_____

_____

_____

_____

_____

_____

_____

_____

THE TOXICITY OF ME

Dear Heavenly Father,

Forgive me for self-medicating. I should have consulted you Father and sought your guidance before getting in another relationship. Forgive me for not giving myself time to heal. I realize that I'm literally polluting any new relationship I have because I haven't healed from my last situation. Give me the courage to seek help. Restore me as only you can. In Jesus' name, Amen.

POINT 10

There Is Hope

We fully understand that the enemy has traps set for us, but we allow loneliness and vulnerability to supersede facts. We break our own rules and compromise; doing things we know are not good for us.

You must realize that you are valuable. To protect your anointing, you must be sober and vigilant at all times. Remember, according to the Word of God, the devil walks around like a roaring lion, seeking anyone he may devour (1 Peter 5:8). The enemy desires to sift us like wheat, destroy us, and put us in a place to where we are constantly oppressed and depressed. But thanks be to God for the scripture that says, "We are troubled on every side, yet not distressed; we are perplexed, but not in despair; Persecuted, but not forsaken; cast down, but not destroyed (2 Corinthians 4:8–9).

Those words are what keep me from day to day. Those words help me to realize that there are lions out to destroy me. However, I serve a God who is a protector, a deliverer. He is a God who will cover me when I am not covering myself. I thank God that he looks out for me. I am more so grateful for an ear to hear God speaking, constantly reminding me that I am his, and he is mine.

We must remain prayerful because depression, loneliness, complacency, and fear can cause us to connect to toxic people if we are not careful. Am I saying that all people are toxic? No, I am not. I am saying that there are toxic people out there, and they are preying on those who have been hurt, are vulnerable, misused, abused, have low self-esteem, are weak willed … Shall I go on? Toxic individuals will not tell you that they are the reason there are twenty-five or more broken people walking around.

When you are in a toxic relationship, you'll find that the person doing the infecting does not care about how broken he or she leaves you. All the individual wants is to milk you dry emotionally and often financially. Now you are left seeking counsel. Hold your head up, and know that you are bruised but not broken! Improve your prayer life. Stick closer to God, and watch him change things. You can be restored.

Father, I confess ...

_____

_____

_____

_____

_____

_____

_____

_____

_____

_____

_____

_____

_____

_____

_____

_____

_____

_____

_____

_____

_____

_____

Dear Heavenly Father,

Your word tells us in Jeremiah 29:11, that you know the plans you have for us to give us a future and hope. Hope is something I need help hold on to. Father, I get weak sometimes and have decided to lean on you much more. When I am tired, I will lean on you. When I am depressed, I will lean on you. When I am frustrated, I will lean on you. Please forgive me for running to other sources other than you, the God who holds my future. I will embrace your unchanging hand all the more. I trust you and know that you will see me through whatever comes my way. Restore me as only you can. In Jesus' name, Amen.

REFERENCES

"Manipulation: 7 Signs to Look For." *WebMD*

www.webmd.com › Mental Health › Reference (accessed November 19, 2020).

Abigail Brenner, "8 Things Most Toxic People in Your Life Have in Common," *Psychology Today*, August 29, 2016.

Cindy Lamothe, "12 Signs of a Controlling. Personality".https:// www.healthline.com/health/controlling-people November 21, 2019

REFERENCES

Printed in the United States
by Baker & Taylor Publisher Services